COLOUR LIBRARY OF SCIENCE
WARM-BLOODED
ANIMALS

COLOUR LIBRARY OF SCIENCE
WARM-BLOODED
ANIMALS

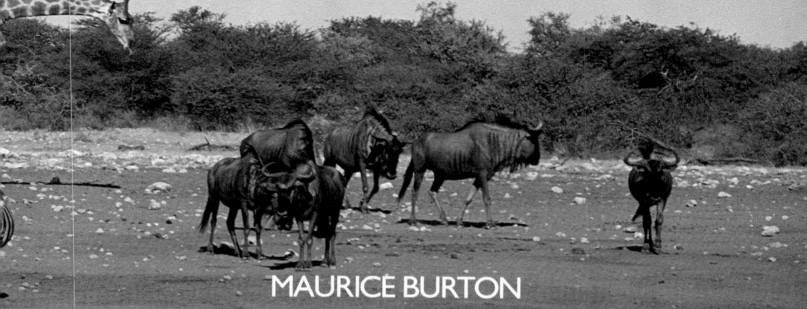

MAURICE BURTON

ORBIS · LONDON

First published in Great Britain by
Orbis Publishing Limited, London 1985

© 1985 Orbis Publishing Limited, London

Printed in Italy
10 9 8 7 6 5 4 3 2 1

Warm-blooded Animals
ISBN: 0–85613–837–1

Previous pages
Giraffes, zebras and
wildebeest gather to
drink at a waterhole in
south-west Africa.

Editor Penny Clarke
Designer Roger Kohn

CONTENTS

Note There are some unusual words in this book. They are explained in the Glossary on pages 62–63. The first time a word is used in the text it is printed in *italics*.

▼The jerboa or desert rat is a distant relative of the common rat. It lives in the deserts of North Africa, burrowing in the sand by day and coming out at night to feed on seeds. It moves by leaps with its long hind legs.

I
WHAT IS A MAMMAL?

A MAMMAL IS ...

There are two kinds of animal that scientists describe as *warm-blooded*: birds and *mammals*. All the rest of the creatures in the animal kingdom are said to be *cold-blooded*.

Warm-blooded animals and cold-blooded animals

The terms 'warm-blooded' and 'cold-blooded' are really rather misleading. In a cold-blooded animal the temperature of its body changes as the temperature of the surrounding air changes. In a warm-blooded animal the temperature of the body remains more or less the same, unless the animal is ill or *hibernating*.

A warm-blooded animal keeps warm because of its coat of hair or fur (or feathers, in the case of birds). In cold weather, or when there is a sudden drop in the temperature of it surroundings, it raises its own temperature by shivering. If the surroundings get too hot, as at midday or in the summer, it can cool itself by sweating or panting.

Dogs, cats, horses, elephants, monkeys and tigers are all examples of warm-

◀ A hibernating dormouse lies curled in a ball. Before going to sleep for the winter it eats heavily and puts on fat. Then, as it falls asleep, its breathing rate and heart beat become so slow the dormouse appears to be dead. It is then cold-blooded. It sleeps so soundly it can be rolled across the top of a table and still will not wake.

blooded animals. Snakes, lizards, tortoises, frogs and toads are all cold-blooded•animals.

There is a special name for warm-blooded animals that are not birds. It is mammals. As well as being warm-blooded, mammals have a number of other things in common. They are usually four-legged, although some, such as humans, stand on two. Usually they are covered in hair. Even whales may have a few hairs around their mouths. Except for the platypus (page 13) and echidna (page 13) of Australia, they give birth to live young. And they all suckle their babies after these are born – that is the babies feed on milk from their mothers.

▼ The head of a killer whale, one of the toothed whales. It is the only whale that kills and eats warm-blooded animals, such as seals and penguins.

► An American opussum with her short-haired babies. The adult's hair is coarse and shaggy, with long guard hairs to make the coat waterproof.

HAIR AND FUR

Hair also plays a part in keeping a mammal's body temperature at an even level. Most of the time it lies flat on the body. In cold weather it can be raised, just as a bird ruffles its feathers when it needs extra warmth. In both cases air is trapped among the hair or the feathers, and this acts as *insulation* against the cold.

The hairs grow out from what are called *follicles* in the skin. Each hair is a long *filament*, hollow at the centre and made up of one or more layers of horn. This horn is the same kind of material that makes up our own finger nails.

Different kinds of hair
Different kinds of hair have different names. When an animal's coat consists of hair that is soft and fine but short it is called fur. When fine, soft hair is long and curly it is called wool, as in a sheep. Then the whole coat is called a fleece.

Tough, stiff hairs, especially when they are long, are called bristles. In some animals the hairs are even tougher and

stronger than bristles. They are then called spines. The spiny anteater and the hedgehog are examples of animals with spines. Very long spines, as in the coat of a porcupine, are called *quills*.

The oddest hair of all must belong to the rhinoceros. The horns on its face are made up of a type of matted hair!

▼ Skin and hair come in very different forms, as these four pictures show. The skin of the rhinoceros is tough and almost hairless. Its fierce-looking horn, on the other hand, is a type of hair.

▲As a rule the hairs in a mammal's coat are so arranged that they shed water downwards from the back and shoulders. In sloths which spend much time hanging upside-down, the reverse is true.

► Quills are a special type of hair. The South American tree porcupine has a coat of quills mixed with hair. Unlike most other porcupines it has a long tail which it can wrap round branches to help it in climbing.

◄ Since the days of the Incas of Peru chinchillas have been hunted for their soft fur which is extremely warm because it has more hairs per square centimetre than any other known animal. Now, however, chinchillas are protected and cannot be caught or hunted.

9

THE SKELETON OF A MAMMAL

Mammals, like birds, reptiles and fishes, are *vertebrates*. That is they have a skeleton of bone that consists of a spine that includes the tail, a skull, a shoulder girdle, ribs, a hip girdle and four limbs. One of the main parts of the skeleton is the spine, or backbone, which is made up of a string of small bones called *vertebrae*.

Clues in a skeleton

As we shall discover later in this book, the skeleton of an animal provides many important clues as to how it should be *classified* and which other animals it is related to. The skeletons of all mammals have two very important clues and tell scientists that even though a horse may not look like a whale, and an elephant may not look like a dormouse, all four are, in fact, mammals. The first clue is that almost all mammals have seven neck vertebrae. Some birds have long necks, others have short ones and, as you would expect, the shorter the neck the fewer the neck vertebrae. But in mammals this is not so. Whales, which have no neck at all, have seven neck vertebrae, all squashed together. Giraffes, with the longest neck of any mammal, still only have seven neck vertebrae, but each one is very long. (Only two mammals are different: the three-toed

▼ Gibbons have extremely long arms, as this skeleton clearly shows. The long arms enable the gibbon to run on all fours, which it can do very quickly, but at the same time it can stay almost upright, which helps it to spot enemies easily.

▶ Notice the differences between this skeleton of a bear and that of the gibbon (**top**). The bear has four limbs of practically equal length and all its bones are much bigger – indicating that it is much larger than the gibbon. The skull, too, is very different, with a large snout, heavy jaws and well developed canine teeth.

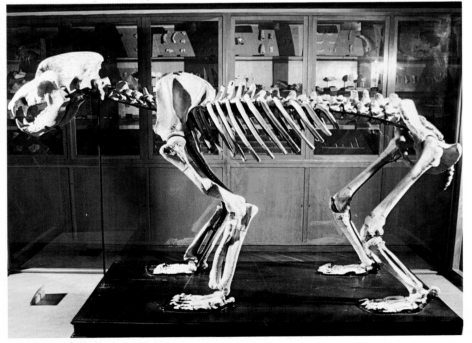

sloth has nine neck vertebrae and the dugong has six.)

The other thing to remember is that the feet of all mammals are *pentadactyl*. This comes from two Greek words meaning 'five fingers'. Although a horse has only one toe, its hoof, scientists know from fossils that its ancestors had five toes on each limb.

Food and teeth

The shape of the teeth in an animal's jaws tells us a great deal about what the animal eats. We are mammals and we have *incisor* teeth in the front of our upper and lower jaws. These are followed by a *canine* tooth on each side in both jaws. After this come the *premolars* and *molars*. Mammals that eat mainly fruit or insects have these four kinds of teeth, too. Those that eat flesh also have the same four kinds, but the canines are much larger. They are used for tearing flesh. Rodents that gnaw their food, for example rats, mice and beavers, have lost the canines but have strong, well-developed incisors. Mammals, such as horses and cows, that eat plants, have large molars.

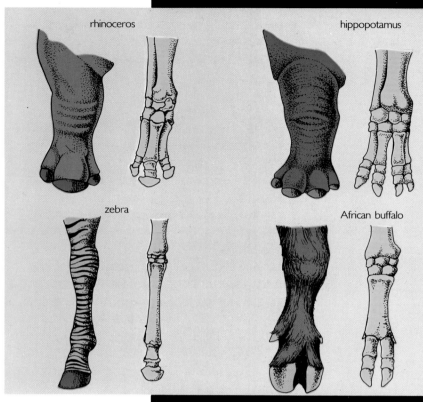

rhinoceros
hippopotamus
zebra
African buffalo

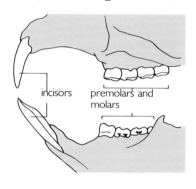

incisors   premolars and molars

◀ Rodents have chisel-like incisors that they use for gnawing. These teeth never stop growing and can only be kept in check by constant use. The front of a rodent's incisor is covered with hard enamel. The back, however, has only soft dentine which wears away faster than the enamel, so forming the tooth's cutting edge.

▲ These drawings show the legs and leg bones of four mammals that no longer have five toes on each limb, although they are all descended from ancestors with five toes. Horses and zebras have only one toe left. Like athletes, they have found speed by always running on their toes.

▼ The five bone 'fingers' in the flippers (yellow) and the tiny hip-bone or pelvic girdle (enlarged at the top of the diagram) tel scientists that whales once lived on land and had limbs like most other mammals.

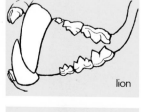

lion

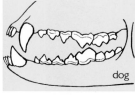

dog

◀ These drawings show the teeth of two carnivores, the lion (top) and the dog (below). These show the small incisors in front, followed by the canines or fangs. The slightly larger carnassial or flesh-teeth can be clearly seen among the premolars and molars of the dog's jaw.

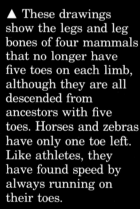

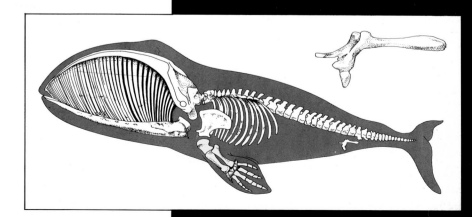

2 DIFFERENT KINDS OF MAMMAL

EGG-LAYING MAMMALS

Platypus

It is not easy to make hard and fast statements about any kind of animal. Although we say mammals bear their young alive there are, in fact, two that do not. Both live in Australia. One is the well-known duckbill or platypus. The other is the spiny anteater, also known as the echidna. Both lay eggs.

The platypus is nearly 60cm (2ft) long, has a furry flattened tail, short legs and a muzzle like a duck's bill. It has tiny eyes and earholes which lie in a groove along each side of its head. These grooves can be closed when the animal is swimming underwater. Its fur is soft and thick, rather like a mole's, and its front feet are webbed. It has five long claws on each front foot and four on each hind foot.

It spends most of its time in water, feeding on worms, crayfish and other small water animals. That is when its webbed feet are useful. When the platypus comes out on land, or when it needs its claws for digging its burrow, it can fold the web back.

When the female is about to lay her eggs she digs a long tunnel in the river bank. She takes care to build walls of earth at intervals along the tunnel, to keep out enemies. She also carries into the tunnel grass and leaves, to make a

◄ The duckbill is found in rivers and lakes in eastern Australia and Tasmania. Its leathery snout, so like the bill of a duck, is very sensitive. It is used for seeking the small animals on which it feeds in the muddy beds of rivers and lakes.

nest, holding these with her tail.

She lays two soft-shelled eggs and protects them and keeps them warm by curling her body around them. The babies hatching from them are naked and blind. They feed by lapping milk that oozes from slits on the mother's belly. At about four months old they are covered with fur like the adults and leave the nest.

Echidna

The echidna, or spiny anteater, is the other exception to the rule that mammals give birth to live young. The female echidna lays only one egg which she then tucks into her pouch – a fold of skin on her belly. There the egg stays until it hatches. The baby from it laps milk in the same way as the baby platypus does.

An adult echidna looks rather like a large hedgehog or a small porcupine. Its rounded body, which may reach 50cm (20in) in length, has no tail and is covered with hair, with many spines poking through on the back. Like the platypus it has tiny eyes and no ear flaps and its muzzle is long and similar to a bird's thin beak. It also has a long thin tongue for mopping up ants and termites, after it has broken open their nests with its strong claws.

When it wants to rest, the echidna digs a burrow. It does this so quickly it seems to be sinking into the ground. Sometimes it just buries itself under a large stone or in a hollow log. It also searches under stones and logs for insects, especially termites and ants.

An echidna can go without food for a month if necessary, and in cold weather it hibernates until the weather gets warmer.

◄ A drawing on a piece of bark made by an Australian aborigine. It is supposed to show one of the many unusual animals in Australia, the echidna or spiny anteater.

► In real life the echidna is almost as odd as the aboriginal artist made it look. Although its looks clumsy it can move quickly. It comes out mainly at night to feed. If disturbed it rolls into a ball of prickles.

▲ When it is born, the baby kangaroo is very small. It climbs through its mother's fur into her pouch and grasps a teat in its mouth. There it stays, feeding, until it is old enough to leave the pouch and hop about on the ground.

There are many kinds of kangaroo in Australia and the nearby islands. The largest of them is the red kangaroo, which may be over 2m (6½ft) tall. The smallest are the rat-kangaroos. The smallest of these is only about 50cm (20in) long, with its tail making up nearly half of that length. In general, small kangaroos are called wallabies.

More marsupials

Another Australian marsupial is the wombat. It has a stocky body about 1m (3ft) long and looks very similar to a badger. In fact Australians often call it a badger. In contrast to the sturdy wombat are the little marsupial mice, which are rarely more than 16cm (6½in) long.

The Tasmanian wolf is extremely rare, indeed it may now be extinct. It looks, or looked, like a large, fierce dog and was carnivorous. Another marsupial *carnivore* is the native cat. These animals hunt at night for their prey of small mammals, birds, lizards, fish and insects.

If the kangaroo is Australia's most famous animal, the koala, sometimes called the koala bear, must come a very close second. Unlike kangaroos and wallabies, its legs are about the same size and it has no tail. It spends most of its time in trees, mainly eucalyptus or gum trees.

Apart from Australia and the islands near it, such as New Guinea, marsupials are found only in America. Most of these live in South America, but the best-known is the American opossum, that also lives in the United States. Some of the Australian marsupials look similar to the American opossum and are called opossums, or possums for short.

▲ Wallabies are a type of small kangaroo and live on the plains of Australia. This female has a well-grown baby in her pouch. It can probably hop quite strongly across country on its own, but like a baby kangaroo, it will return to the mother's pouch if disturbed or frightened.

Australia is also the home of other unusual animals. These are the pouched mammals or marsupials. The word marsupial comes from the Latin word *marsuppium* meaning 'pouch'. And although marsupial animals look very different from one another they all have one thing in common: the females carry their babies in a pouch.

Kangaroos

The kangaroo is possibly the best known of all Australian animals. It is a marsupial. It has long strong hind legs and very small front legs. Instead of running it takes long leaps with the hind legs. When not going for long distances, it hops along on its hind legs. When it rests it does so on its hind feet using its long strong tail as a prop. The female kangaroo carries her baby, known as a joey, in a pouch on her belly.

▶ One of the most colourful marsupials is the spotted cuscus of New Guinea and other islands north-east of Australia. It is the size of a large cat, lives in trees and wraps its tail round the branches to support itself. It comes out at night to feed on leaves. When disturbed it makes loud, cross swearing noises.

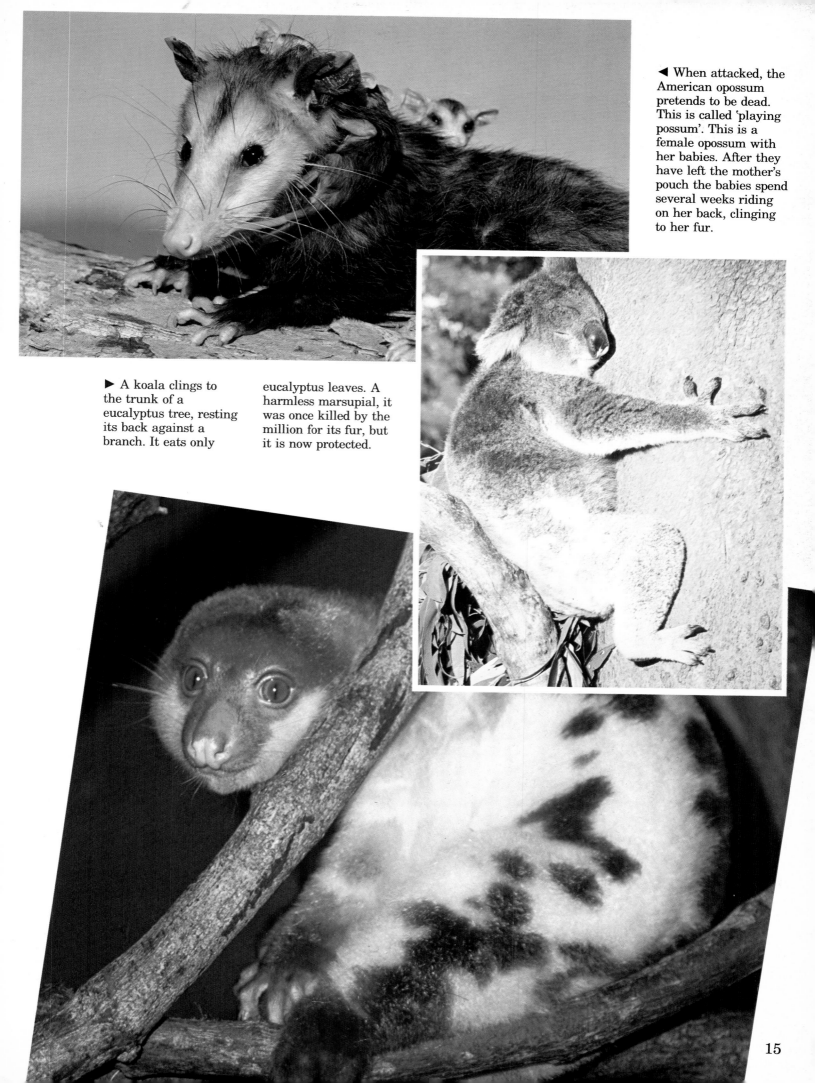

◄ When attacked, the American opossum pretends to be dead. This is called 'playing possum'. This is a female opossum with her babies. After they have left the mother's pouch the babies spend several weeks riding on her back, clinging to her fur.

► A koala clings to the trunk of a eucalyptus tree, resting its back against a branch. It eats only eucalyptus leaves. A harmless marsupial, it was once killed by the million for its fur, but it is now protected.

INSECTIVORES

▲ Shrews are among the smallest of mammals. They look like mice but they have smaller ears and tiny eyes. They feed on insects, finding them with their long whiskers and keen sense of smell.

Among the smallest of mammals are those known as *insectivores*. This name comes from the Latin and means 'insect-eaters'. That does not mean that they all eat nothing but insects. One of the best-known is the hedgehog, which will eat slugs, snails, worms, mice, rats, frogs, lizards and even snakes. Then there are moles that live almost entirely on earthworms.

The reason why scientists group together animals as different as these is because their teeth are so alike. Each has many small teeth beginning with the incisors in the front of the mouth. These are followed by a canine tooth and then by premolars and molars. Each cheek

tooth has points, known as *cusps*, which are just the thing for catching and crushing hard insects, although they can also be used for softer foods.

In their search for food, and especially when they are searching for insects, these animals probe under stones, in the earth or under dead leaves. So they all have long sensitive snouts. Some shrews living in Africa are known as elephant shrews because their snout is like a short trunk.

Big and little

The largest insectivore, the otter shrew, lives in West Africa. It is 60cm (2ft) long, from the tip of its nose to the tip of its tail and, as its name suggests, looks like a small otter. Its home is in mountain streams where it probes among pebbles on the stream bed for water insects.

The smallest insectivore is another shrew, known as Savi's white-toothed shrew. It is only 33mm (1¼in) long, including its tail. It is the smallest living mammal. Years ago, in the main hall of the Natural History Museum in London, there was a stuffed African elephant. This is the largest living land mammal.

▼ Moles spend their time underground. But, like this European mole, occasionally come to the surface. You can see clearly its tapering snout and its broad front feet.

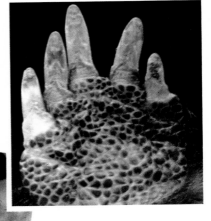

▲ The mole's broad front paws, with their long strong claws, are a kind of pick and shovel all in one. They are used to dig away the soil and pass it back to the small hind feet to push out of the way.

In life it would have weighed about 6 tonnes (6½ tons). On the floor, between its huge feet, was a Savi's white-toothed shrew. In life this would have weighed less than 6g (⅙oz).

By comparison, the pygmy shrew of the United States is almost large. It measures 69mm (2¾in) and weighs 28.5g (1oz).

As you might expect, such tiny animals do not live long. The common shrew of Europe, 112mm (4½in) long, reaches extreme old age at 15 months. As a result, shrews can often be found lying dead on footpaths in late summer. This gave rise, in medieval times, to the belief that a shrew could not cross a human footpath and live.

◄ The solenodon is an insectivore found only on the West Indian islands of Cuba and Haiti. It is like a shrew but much larger, nearly 60cm (2ft) long, although nearly half of this is tail.

The mother of the baby hedgehogs (**above**) must have been disturbed, because normally they do not come into the open while they are still blind and as helpless as these ones are. Once they are old enough and strong enough, the female takes her young out to learn to hunt and forage for themselves (**left**).

BATS – FLYING INSECT HUNTERS

▶ The long-eared bat hovers around trees for the insects living there. Its sensitive echo-location system enables it to locate insects and pick them off the leaves.

▲ The horse-shoe bat has sharp teeth with which to crunch up the tough wing-cases of the beetles and other insects that it eats.

▼ This diagram shows how the bat's echo-location works. The white dots show the sound waves travelling from the bat's mouth and striking a solid object, then being bounced back to the bat's ear. The bat makes a mental picture of its surroundings from the echoes.

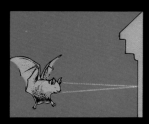

If bats did not have wings they would almost certainly have been classified as insectivores. Their teeth are very similar to the teeth of insectivores and most of them feed only on insects. They are the only mammals able to fly in the same way as birds: by beating the air with their wings.

A bat's wing is, however, totally unlike that of a bird. To start with it has no feathers and its bone structure is different. In the bat's wing the forearm has grown very long and so have the four fingers. A thin skin stretches across these fingers and also runs down each side of the body to the hind limbs. Usually it encloses the tail as well. The thumb is short and has a strong claw at its tip. This is used for climbing.

The toes of the hind limbs are long and each has a long curved claw at the tip. The bat uses these for hanging from a support while resting. It also uses them for combing its fur.

Many bats catch insects in the air, coming out from their daytime resting places to hunt in the early evening. Others, for example the long-eared bat,

pick them off the leaves of trees as they hover. And, unlike many insectivores, they have short snouts. Most bats have folds of bare skin, known as *nose-leaves*, on their noses.

Hunting by echo-location

Another striking difference between bats and insectivores is that many different kinds of bat hunt by what is called *echo-location*. Although some insect-eating bats pick insects off the leaves of trees, most do not. It is these bats that use echo-location to find their insect prey as they hunt during the fading light of the early evening. While these bats are hunting they make sounds so high-pitched that we cannot hear them. When these sounds strike a solid object they are bounced back as echoes. The bat's ears pick up these echoes and the bat can tell whether the echoes come from an insect or from something solid in their path that must be avoided.

Bats are not blind, whatever the expression 'Blind as a bat' might make you think, but their eyes are very small. This is no disadvantage, because they can find their way in the dark using their echo-location.

Fruit-eating bats

Fruit-eating bats occur in Africa, Malaysia and Australasia. They have much larger eyes than insect-eating bats, suggesting that they rely more on their sight for finding food and places to roost than the insect-eating bats. Fruit-eating bats are larger than insect-eating bats. The largest, known as flying foxes, live mainly in south-east Asia. Their wings span nearly 2m (5ft). This is a marked contrast to the hog-nosed, or bumble bee, bat of Thailand. This bat was discovered in 1975 and has a wingspan of 16cm (6in).

Other kinds of bat, that eat *pollen* and *nectar* live in South America, Malaysia and Australasia. Many of these bats have a slow, hovering flight and do not use echo-location to find their food, which is, after all, stationary.

▲ This photograph shows one of the more common bats, the pipistrelle, in flight. The bones of the four long fingers that support the wing can be seen clearly in the right wing. The thumb is represented by the claw on the angle of the wing. The pipistrelle comes out at dusk to hunt flying insects.

▶ A bat roosting in a cave, its wings wrapped around its body. The bone 'fingers' that support the wings are clearly visible through the thin skin.

▶ A group of flying foxes rests in a tree. These are fruit-eating bats. Not only do they eat large quantities of fruit, but their droppings sometimes damage the foliage of the trees.

MONKEYS AND APES – OUR NEAREST RELATIVES

Two hundred years ago monkeys and apes were classified with bats. Although this now seems extraordinary, remember that very few Europeans had actually seen many monkeys and apes in the wild. Classifying animals, deciding which kinds of animals are related to one another, is based mainly on the study of skeletons and skins kept in museums. And if you look into the mouths of monkeys and apes, their teeth are very similar to those of bats and insectivores, such as shrews, moles and hedgehogs.

Now, however, monkeys and apes are put in a separate group, together with lemurs. This group is called the *primates*, from the Latin word meaning 'first'. The reason for calling them by this name is that they have a brain of the first rank. In other words, they are the most intelligent of all animals. We human beings are also classified with monkeys and apes.

The lemurs (the loris, tarsier and potto are all lemurs) are sometimes called half-monkeys because they are only halfway to being monkeys. They are, for example, not as intelligent. Monkeys and apes, on the other hand, are so very like us that it is not hard to think of them almost as cousins. This is because they, like us, have large brains. And, like us, they use their forelimbs as hands. Monkeys, apes and humans can think and can use tools. Although sea otters and some birds use stones or sticks as tools, research suggests that primates use tools for more varied tasks.

Food for primates

The first primates to appear on earth almost certainly ate insects. They also ate leaves and fruit. There are some kinds of monkey that eat nothing but leaves. Even the mighty gorilla, at 1.7m (5½ft) the largest of the man-like apes, eats only vegetation. The chimpanzee is smaller than the gorilla, reaching a height of about 1.5m (4½ft). It is the most human-looking of the primates. Although it eats mainly fruit, it will also eat vegetables. It has been seen to eat insects and also kill and eat small animals such as birds, and even small monkeys.

▲ The mountain gorilla of West Africa is the largest of the apes. Although larger than a man, and stronger, it eats only plant food and is remarkably peaceful.

◄ Chimpanzees often use tools. They will use sticks to get honey from a comb, or to dig ants or termites from their nests.

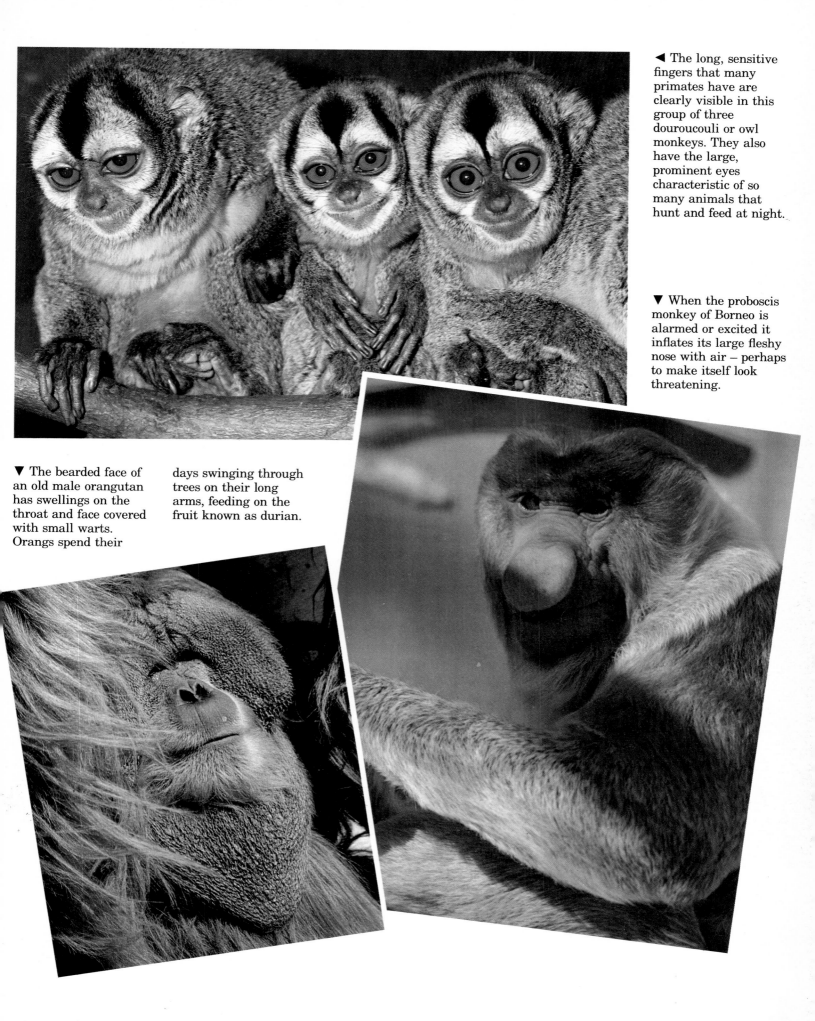

◀ The long, sensitive fingers that many primates have are clearly visible in this group of three douroucouli or owl monkeys. They also have the large, prominent eyes characteristic of so many animals that hunt and feed at night.

▼ When the proboscis monkey of Borneo is alarmed or excited it inflates its large fleshy nose with air – perhaps to make itself look threatening.

▼ The bearded face of an old male orangutan has swellings on the throat and face covered with small warts. Orangs spend their days swinging through trees on their long arms, feeding on the fruit known as durian.

THE TOOTHLESS ONES

So far we have said a good deal about the teeth of mammals and their importance in showing which kinds of mammal are related to one another. Now we come to those that have no teeth or have only small and very weak teeth. This group includes the anteaters, sloths and armadillos of America. The scientific name for these three kinds of animal is

▼ The three-toed sloth, or unau, lives in trees in the dense forests of South America. It feeds on the leaves and flowers of the cecropia tree, a kind of mulberry.

▲ The nine-banded armadillo is one of 20 species living in South America. During this century it has been moving north into parts of the United States. Because it is heavily armoured it cannot move quickly out of the way of large vehicles and often is killed under their wheels on the main highways.

▲ The tamandua lives in Central America and also on the island of Trinidad. It feeds on ants that make their nests in trees. Its tail is prehensile. That is, it can be wrapped round a branch to hold the tamandua steady while it is tearing open an ant's nest with the large claws on its front feet.

Edentata. This is from a Latin word and means 'without teeth' or toothless.

Exceptions to every rule

As you will have realised by now, nothing is straightforward in studying animals. Whenever scientists think they have found a rule, important exceptions to it will soon be discovered. This is especially true for the edentates. For instance, the anteaters have no teeth at all. The sloths have a few molars in the back of the mouth, and so have some of the armadillos. Their molars are, however, small and weak and they have no enamel. In most armadillos there are a dozen or so teeth in each jaw, but in the giant armadillo there may be 100 in the whole mouth. There is, in fact, only one thing similar about the teeth of this group of animals: not one of them has any teeth in the front of the mouth.

Different food and different teeth

The differences in these animals' teeth are reflected in the food they eat. Anteaters eat only ants and termites, both soft-bodied insects. The sloths, well-known for hanging upside-down from branches, eat only leaves and fruit. The armadillos also eat insects, but they will eat earthworms and small *reptiles*, as well as eggs, fruit and leaves, and even the flesh of small dead animals.

Are they really related?

So why are the anteaters, sloths and armadillos grouped together? The Edentata are, in fact, a good example of how scientists group animals together. Animals that look alike are not always related, and animals that look very different can be related. In this group are anteaters with hairy bodies and long tubular snouts. The sloths have a coat of coarse hair and a very short snout. And, in even greater contrast, the armadillos have long snouts but bodies covered with horny plates. So the three kinds of animal look very different. Yet the similarities in their skeletons show that they are related.

Anteaters with a difference

There are two kinds of animals that used to be classified with the edentates. They are the pangolins and the aardvarks. Both eat ants or termites. Pangolins have bodies covered in horny plates and no teeth at all. The aardvark has no teeth in the front of its mouth. So you can understand why scientists at first thought they were related to the Edentata. However, closer study of their skeletons showed that they are not closely related

to anteaters, sloths and armadillos, so now they are each classified in a group of their own.

The ant-eating pig

There is only one species of aardvark or, as it is sometimes called, the ant-bear or earth-pig. It is found throughout Africa south of the Sahara. Its head, which is long and narrow, ends in a pig-like snout and a small mouth. The aardvark uses its long tongue to sweep up ants and termites, after breaking open their nests with its strong claws. There are four claws on the front feet and five on each hind foot.

Ants and termites can be troublesome when their nests have been disturbed. Those not swept up by the aardvark's tongue swarm over its snout. They would crawl into its nostrils except that the aardvark can open and close them at will. As a further defence to keep the insects out, the edges of the nostrils are protected by short, stiff bristles.

It is a shy animal and comes out mainly at night. Because of this little was known about it, and for a long time scientists thought it was an edentate. Now, however, they know it is not.

► The pig-like aardvark of Africa is 2m (6½ft) long, weighs 64kg (140lb), has a tail 60cm (2ft) long and a long thin tongue 45cm (18in) long. Its teeth, which have no enamel and so are weak, are quite unlike the teeth of any known living animal.

RABBITS, HARES AND PIKAS

▲ Hares have longer hind legs and longer ears than rabbits. Also, hares do not burrow. The animal shown here is the black-tailed jack rabbit. Compare this picture with the cottontail (**right**) and the European rabbit (**opposite**) and you will see that the animal is, in fact, a hare, in spite of its name.

It is not so many years ago that rabbits and hares were thought of as rodents, close relatives of rats, mice and squirrels. This was largely because they all are gnawing animals. That is, they have a pair of long incisors in both upper and lower jaws. It had, however, been noted that rabbits and hares have a second incisor, a very small one, close behind each incisor in the upper jaw. These second incisors are so small that they seemed unimportant. Then scientists looked very closely at the skeletons of these two kinds of animal and saw many differences. In 1945 the American scientist, Dr Gaylord Simpson, suggested they should be put into two groups. Now rabbits and hares, and another kind of mammal, the pika, are grouped together and called the *Lagomorpha*. This name is from two Greek words and means 'shaped like a hare'. In other words members of this group have long hind legs, long ears and a very short tail, often called the scut.

Now we come to another exception to the rule. Pikas do look rather like rabbits, but they have short ears, all four legs of equal length and no tail. There are only a few species of them. One lives in the Rocky Mountains of North America, the others live in the mountains of Asia. They are small, the largest being

▲ The cottontail of the United States is also called a molly or briar rabbit. The smallest, the desert cottontail, shown here, burrows in the sand. Its fur blends with the sand of the desert.

only 17.5cm (7in) long. The Mount Everest pika that lives on the slopes of Mount Everest lives at nearly 6,000m (17,500ft), the highest altitude for a mammal.

Rabbits and hares usually live in the lowlands, especially where there are wide stretches of grass, on which they feed. The European rabbit breeds fast and frequently and can do enormous damage to crops. It was taken to Australia, where it had no natural enemies, and within a short time it became a plague, eating the grass on which the great herds of cattle and flocks of sheep grazed.

When is a hare a rabbit?
Hares do not burrow in the ground. Yet they are so like rabbits in other ways that sometimes they are called rabbits. This is true of the hares of North America, which are called Jack rabbits. On the whole, if it has long hind legs and long ears it is called a hare. If the hind legs are not so long and the ears shorter then it is called a rabbit. Otherwise there is little difference between the two

names. For instance, the marsh hare of North America is also called the marsh rabbit and the swamp rabbit is also called the marsh hare.

One of the rarest of all rabbits and hares must be the Nelson hare or Mexican pygmy rabbit. It is found only on the slopes of two volcanoes in Mexico, Popocatepetl and Izaccihyatl.

▼ European rabbits originally lived only in south-west Europe. They then started to spread northwards. Early men took rabbits with them as they, too, moved north. Later, rabbits were taken to Australia. Wherever it goes it is a pest to grass and other crops.

▶ Hares living in cold regions have a brown coat in summer. In winter their coat is white so that they are hard to see against the snow. The change from brown to white comes with the moult, when the brown hairs are replaced by new, white hairs.

EVER-HUNGRY RODENTS

▲ Hamsters make popular pets. This golden hamster at its food bowl has stuffed its cheek pouches with food. It will go back to its nest, empty the pouches and store the food. Although pets should not need to store food, in the wild it is a habit essential for survival.

There are around 4,000 kinds of mammals. About two-thirds of these are rodents, known also as gnawing animals. Rodents fall into three groups: squirrels and beavers, porcupines and rats and mice. Of these the rats and mice are by far the most numerous. There are more species and the numbers in each species are far greater. Think, for instance, of the numbers of household rats there are in the world. In any one country these common rats are more numerous than people. As if to make matters worse there are often plagues of them, when the rats suddenly appear, as if from nowhere, in their tens of thousands.

It is not surprising that in such a large group of animals there is a great range of sizes. The smallest rodent is probably the northern pygmy mouse of the southern United States and Mexico, which measures about 13cm (5in) including the tail. The harvest mouse of northern Europe and Asia is almost as small. In contrast to these tiny rodents is the capybara of South and Central America, which measures 1.25m (4ft). This is even bigger than the giant rats of New Guinea, which are nearly 1m (3ft) long.

Dangerous pests
Rodents as a whole are looked upon as pests. They eat only plant food and so are a menace to crops. By their constant gnawing and burrowing some of them are a nuisance through the damage they do to buildings and to river banks. Moreover, some of them carry diseases. The most outstanding instance of rodents carrying disease is the Black Death, or bubonic plague, carried by black rats, which in some places in Europe in the Middle Ages killed nine people out of every ten.

Not all rodents, however, are unpopular pests. Some of our favourite pets have been rodents. White mice and white rats were popular for a long time. Their place has now been taken by hamsters and gerbils. And of course, the guinea pig has been popular for a long time. Guinea pigs are native to South America. They were domesticated by the Incas of Peru. The

▼The North American porcupine lives in wooded areas of the United States and Canada. It feeds on twigs, leaves and buds. It has hollow spines, or quills, growing among the hair covering its body.

▲ Gerbils come from the desert and semi-desert regions of Africa and Asia, particularly around the Sahara desert. They feed on plants and often store food in their burrows.

▲ Young red squirrels of Europe and Asia live mainly in pine woods. They feed on pine seeds, nuts, fungi and insects. The nest, made of twigs, is known as a drey.

◄ The largest of living rodents is the capybara of South America. As large as a pig, it lives on the banks of lakes and rivers, feeding on water plants. With its webbed feet it is an agile swimmer.

first Europeans to reach South America brought guinea pigs back with them and since then they have been taken all over the world.

Teeth of destruction

The destructiveness of rodents springs almost entirely from the kind of teeth they have. Like rabbits and hares, rodents have two pairs of incisors in the front of the mouth. The incisors of rabbits and hares have a layer of enamel on both the front and the back. Rodents have enamel only on the front of the incisors.

As they chew, the soft dentine at the back of the tooth wears away, so each incisor becomes like a chisel, with a sharp cutting edge. That is why rats are able to chew through lead pipes and even through concrete. Squirrels, which are also rodents, chew metal objects, such as lead labels in gardens. Porcupines can chew glass bottles and beavers fell trees using only their teeth.

WILD DOGS

It is highly likely that the first animal to be domesticated by humans was the dog. This may have taken place 10,000 years ago. Certainly dogs were 'companions of man' before the horse and the cat, but it was so long ago that we can only guess how it came about.

◀ A North American wolf stands and howls on a look-out rock. This cry can be heard over great distances and is a frightening, eerie sound. To wolves it is a signal that they are about to gather before setting off to hunt. To their prey it is a warning that there is danger about.

▲ The thick coat of the Arctic fox provides both protection against the cold and good camouflage.

◀ A European red fox photographed in a wood at autumn. The shading of its coat blends well with the browns and greys of the woodlands, providing an excellent camouflage.

◀ Two coyotes scavenge the remains of a carcase. The coyote, or prairie wolf, is a smaller cousin of the wolf and looks very like it. Coyotes hunt singly or in pairs, seldom in groups as do wolves. They also hunt smaller animals. They will eat plant food, such as fruit or vegetables, and carrion.

Prehistoric man must have been surrounded by wild dogs of many kinds, such as wolves, foxes and jackals. These, together with the few we still call 'wild dogs', make up the dog family. They feed on flesh although most of them also eat small amounts of fruit and vegetation. They catch large prey by running it down then snapping at it when it is exhausted. Some species, such as foxes, hunt singly. But most dogs hunt in packs. Jackals usually hunt on their own, like foxes, but will sometimes come together in packs.

The domestic dog is believed to be descended from the wolf, which lives in the northern parts of the northern hemisphere. Adult male wolves are about 80cm (31½in) high at the shoulder and reach a length of 140cm (4½ft), excluding the tail. The coyote, also known as the prairie wolf, lives in North America. It is very like a wolf but smaller.

Another member of the dog family is the jackal, which lives in warmer countries, in Africa and southern Asia. This, too, is very like a wolf but, at about 100cm (40in) long, including the tail, it is not much bigger than the largest fox. The dingo, the wild dog of Australia, is a domesticated dog taken to Australia by the Aborigines which then went wild.

The strongest of the dog family is the Cape hunting dog of the southern half of Africa. It is about the size of a wolf and very powerfully built. It hunts in packs, the dogs keeping in touch by hooting softly instead of barking.

The smaller members of the dog family are the foxes. The largest is the red fox of Europe and North America. The smallest, the fennec of the deserts of Africa and Arabia, weighs only 1.5kg (3-4lb), about half the size of the red fox. It has large

ears, like those of the bat-eared fox living on sandy plains of South and East Africa.

The teeth of a hunter
Whatever the size of the animal and however much the wild dogs and foxes differ in shape or colour, all have the same kind of teeth. In the front of the mouth are the incisors. These teeth are used for picking up small prey. Behind them are the fangs, or canines, for holding large prey or for making slashing cuts. Then come the cheek teeth, made up of premolars and molars.

The dog family are carnivores, a word which means flesh-eaters. One cheek tooth on each side of both upper and lower jaws is much enlarged and has a prominent cutting edge. These are called *carnassials* or flesh-teeth. They are used for cutting flesh once a piece has been taken into the mouth.

▼ In Australia lives the dingo or wild dog. But is it a truly wild dog? The Aborigines reached Australia from Asia several thousand years ago and scientists believe they brought the dingo with them. Some of these domesticated dingos escaped and went back to living in the wild. Today's dingos are their descendants.

BEARS

Bears are lumbering tail-less animals with broad flat feet. They are short-sighted but their sense of smell and their hearing is good. There are eight different kinds of bears, most of them found only in the northern hemisphere. The largest is the polar bear, 3m (9½ft) long and weighing over 500kg (1,300lb). The smallest is the Malayan bear, also called the sun bear, of south-east Asia, from Burma to Borneo. It is little more than 1m (3½ft) long.

Except for the polar bear, which is white, bears are either brown or black, and live in wild mountainous country or in forests. The polar bear feeds on seals, stalking them over the ice, or waiting beside holes in the ice for a seal to come up for air. The others feed on berries and other wild fruits as well as small animals living under stones. They will also eat fish, scooping them out of shallow rivers with a flip of the paw. Bears also love honey, taken from the nests of wild bees.

The teeth of bears are like those of dogs except that the cheek-teeth are weak and have flattened surfaces. The larger bears, such as the grizzly, will occasionally kill and eat animals larger than themselves, such as caribou. They kill with a single blow of one of their large front paws. Even human beings are sometimes killed by a *rogue* bear. That is, one that is not behaving as it should. Arctic explorers have to be constantly on the alert for polar bears. There are many records of these bears, which can move extremely fast across the ice, attacking humans.

Bears, especially brown and black bears, can climb well although they do so slowly, making sure each bough will bear their weight. They will climb mountains then slide down or come down head-over-heels.

A winter sleep

Dogs and foxes can stand up to cold weather but bears go into a sleep called hibernation for the winter. But, unlike chipmunks, dormice and some bats that hibernate, a hibernating bear can be roused from its sleep. The polar bear does not hibernate but a she-bear will go into a hole deep in the snow to have her babies, during the winter. Brown and black bears sleep during the winter and the females have their babies then. They sleep in caves, in holes between rocks, in large hollow logs or between the roots of large trees.

Baby bears are surprisingly small when first born. A mother bear weighing over ½ tonne will give birth to 1–4 babies each weighing only 450g (1lb). At first the babies look like shapeless lumps of flesh. The mother licks them clean and they soon begin to grow and to look like little bears. In fact early naturalists believed that the she-bear really did lick her babies into shape. But that was because a she-bear with cubs is fierce and aggressive, and it was difficult to get close enough to see the newly-born cubs.

▼ A two-year-old grizzly bear with a salmon it has found stranded on a bank. Brown bears eat mainly fruits, roots and such plant foods, as well as small animals living under stones. The grizzly goes to the streams where there are salmon and flips the fish out of the water with its paw.

◀ The largest of all grizzly bears are the Kodiak bears that live on the island of Kodiak, off Alaska. They may be over 3m (9½ft) long and weigh well over 450kg (1,000 lb). At most, grizzlys are 400kg (900 lb) and just under 3m (9½ft) long.

▼ Polar bears may be 3m (9½ft) long and weigh 400kg (900 lb) Their favourite prey is seals. A polar bear will stalk a seal making use of hummocks of snow. They are strong swimmers and have been seen swimming well away from the nearest land.

PANDAS AND RACCOONS

► The common, or lesser, panda, is also called the 'cat bear'. Ranging from the eastern Himalayas to western China, it is more common than the giant panda.

▼ The giant panda is one of the world's rarest animals, found only in damp bamboo forests in parts of eastern Tibet and south-west China (**inset map**). Giant pandas live solitary lives, except in the mating season, unlike the common panda which lives in family groups.

If you were asked to name an animal that was almost unheard-of outside China until 50 years ago and is now world-famous what would be your answer? To give a few more clues, it is shaped like a bear, is white with black legs and has black rings round its eyes. It is, of course, the giant panda, now the symbol of the World Wildlife Fund. It was unknown, except to the Chinese, until 1869. Then a French missionary, Père David, bought a panda skin and sent it to France.

The giant panda

The giant panda has teeth like a flesh-eater except that the cheek-teeth have flattened surfaces. Yet it eats mainly bamboo shoots although it will sometimes catch fish, flipped out of water with the paw, as well as rodents and small birds. It is called the 'beishung' by the Chinese, a name which means white bear. Scientists are still not sure whether it is truly a bear or merely looks like one.

The name 'panda' was first given to an animal living in mountain forests of Nepal, southern China and Upper Burma. It is cat-like, nearly 120cm (4ft) long, with a rich chestnut fur, black legs and underside and bushy tail. It is sometimes called a red cat-bear. When the giant panda had been found this smaller animal became known as the lesser panda. It eats leaves and fruit.

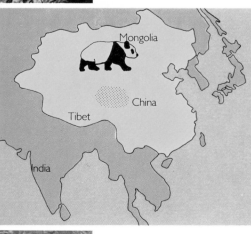

◄ Giant pandas, like many other animals are threatened by humans destroying the places where they live. Once ranging over quite a wide area of Tibet and China, they are now largely confined to the spotted area.

Raccoons

Another famous member of the same family is the raccoon of North America. It is 70cm (2½ft) long with a greyish-brown fur but its tail is ringed and, like the lesser panda, it has black and white markings on its face. It eats mainly water animals such as fish, crayfish and shellfish. Its fingers are long and slender and it is said to be able to untie knots. It is noted for washing its food, even if this is fish or frogs taken from water.

Not quite raccoons

Three other animals, all from the American continent, complete the family. All three live in trees and look like raccoons in build. One is the cacomistle or ringtailed cat. Like the raccoon it comes out at night. It feeds on small birds, rodents, insects and fruit. The second, the coati, or coatimundi, will walk with its ringed tail erect and curled over at the tip. The third, the kinkajou, is famous for using its tail like a monkey to hang from a branch. It will then climb up its own tail to get back onto the branch.

◄ The raccoon is a well-known North American relative of the pandas. The photograph shows its sensitive paws which it frequently uses to wash its food.

► The long pointed nose of the coatimundi is in marked contrast to the short snout of the giant panda (**opposite**). The coatimundi lives mainly on insects and birds' eggs.

◄ The kinkajou lives high in the trees of the forests of Central and South America. About 1m (3ft) in length, it has dense yellow-brown fur, and a long strong tail. It hunts at night.

THE WEASEL FAMILY

The members of the weasel family are carnivorous. Small in size, they are extremely dangerous to the animals they prey on. The weasel, from which the family takes its name, is a little brown animal less than 30cm (1ft) long. The least weasel of northern polar regions is even smaller, seldom more than 23cm (9in) long. Both have very short legs and worm their way through the grass to catch mice, rats, voles, moles, small birds and rabbits. Swift, agile and good climbers, they are relentless killers.

The stoat is slightly larger about 41cm (16in) long. It, too, has a brown coat, but it also has a black tip to its tail. In cold countries the stoat's brown fur turns white in winter, all except for the black

▲ The weasel is a fierce carnivore and a swift, agile killer. A good climber, it raids birds' nests. Unlike its larger relative, the stoat, a weasel does not have a black tip to its tail or turn white in winter.

► Although shy and secretive, the European badger is adapting to living closer to human habitation. This pair live on the western outskirts of London.

► Most otters hunt in freshwater. The sea-otter (**below**) is an exception. It will use stones to crack open shellfish carried on its stomach.

tip to the tail. The stoat's fur, taken in winter, is known as *ermine*.

Related to stoat and weasel, and much the same shape, are the polecat, mink and marten. They also feed on the same kind of prey. The polecat keeps to the ground. The mink hunts on the ground, but will also climb trees to follow its prey. It will also swim to catch fish. Martens hunt in the trees.

There is a kind of domesticated polecat, known as the ferret, which is white with pink eyes. It was used for catching animal pests such as rats and rabbits.

The largest of the weasel family is the wolverine, also known as the glutton. It is just over 1m (3½ft) long. It will kill and eat almost anything it meets, even deer. The glutton is said to fear nothing. It is

so strong it will drag a carcass three times its own weight over rough ground.

All these animals look much alike and there is one other thing they share. When danger threatens they all squirt an extremely nasty smelling liquid from glands near the base of their tail. This habit gives a clue as to which family the skunk belongs.

Otters and badgers also belong to the weasel family. Badgers come out at night and eat almost anything they can find. The honey badger, of Africa, Arabia and India, is especially fond of raiding the nests of wild bees. Otters hunt mainly in water. They feed on fish and frogs but will take almost any small animal.

Mongooses live on land. They look like otters and hunt like the weasel family. But this is another good example of how careful scientists must be when classifying animals. Because there are anatomical differences between members of the weasel family and the mongooses, mongooses are put in a family on their own, together with civets and genets.

▲ The black-and-white markings of the skunk act as a warning to animals that might attack it. When threatened or attacked it produces a foul-smelling liquid in self-defence.

◄ The wolverine is one of the fiercest hunters of the northern forests and Arctic tundra regions. It will cover great distances in its search for food.

▼ Although hyenas look like dogs, their nearest relations are the civets, cat-like relatives of the mongooses (**bottom left**). The best known of the hyenas is the

spotted, also known as the laughing hyena. Its call is said to sound like a man laughing. This group of hyenas is scavenging the carcase of an animal probably killed by lions.

◄ A group of striped mongooses out hunting. Mongooses live in Africa and Asia. These small carnivores will attack poisonous snakes.

CATS IN THE WILD

The last, but by no means the least, of the carnivores is the cat family. The lion, king of beasts, has long appeared on the coats-of-arms of kings and noblemen. To a lesser extent, so has the leopard. At the other end of the scale for size, is the household cat, the domestic pussy, which rivals the dog for human affection and popularity.

The main differences between cats and dogs are that cats can sheathe their claws. Dogs cannot. We say that a cat's claws are *retractile*. Cats also have shorter muzzles than dogs, with the exception, of course, of breeds such as the pug or the bulldog.

All cats are carnivores and the animals they hunt depend on their own size. The smaller cats, such as the European wild cat, the bush cat of Africa and the jungle cat of North Africa and southern Asia, prey on small birds, rodents, and other small animals. The big cats, such as the lion and tiger, kill hoofed animals such as buffalo and large antelopes. Middle-sized cats, such as the leopard of Africa and Asia, and the jaguar of South America, kill middle-sized prey – deer and antelopes.

The lynx is a middle-sized cat with a short tail. Different kinds live in Europe, Asia and North America. One lynx, found throughout the United States, is called a bobcat. All lynxes have tufted ears. They do not run well but have very broad feet and can walk long distances without getting tired.

The fastest runner in the cat family is the cheetah, now found only in Africa. It used also to be common in southern Asia, but has been killed off there. It has a coat covered with small spots and very long legs. Most cats stalk their prey and catch it with a last pounce. Or else they ambush it. Cheetahs, however, run down their prey, reaching speeds of 97kph (60mph) as they do so.

Dogs, too, run down their prey. A cheetah is halfway between cats and dogs in another way – its claws are only partly retractile.

▲ The leopard is the most agile of the Big Cats. It often climbs trees, to rest stretched out along a branch. It also climbs to take the remains of its prey out of reach of hyenas and lions, usually after having eaten enough for one meal.

▲ The puma, or cougar, of America, is also called the mountain lion. It looks like a lioness and is about the same size.

▲Because we think of tigers as animals living in hot countries, it is rather surprising to discover that they love lying in water, especially in the midday heat. The answer is that tigers originated in the temperate regions of Asia, where the winters are long and the ground covered in snow for much of the year. As a result they cannot stand too much heat.

▼ The lion was once common throughout all of Africa, most of southern Asia, and even parts of southern Europe. Second only to the tiger in size, it is one of the Big Cats, the other three being the tiger, the leopard and the jaguar. Only the male lion has a mane; the lioness has short hair over the whole body.

▼ The lynx, which is also a member of the cat family, has a stumpy tail and tufted ears. The lynx shown here is known as the bobcat. It lives in North America. All lynxes are tireless walkers as they follow their prey.

SEALS — SEA-DWELLING CARNIVORES

► Sealions are found on the Pacific coasts of North and South America, on the coasts of Australia, the Auckland Islands (south of New Zealand) and Japan. They, and the fur seals, are known as eared seals. But their ears are very small, as this photograph shows.

► A baby harp seal on an icefloe in the North Atlantic. The attractive fur of these baby seals has led to them being widely hunted, although the increasing awareness of conservation is helping to reduce the hunting.

▼ The largest of all seals is the elephant seal. It was given this name not so much for its size as for the long drooping nose of the male. A bull elephant seal may be nearly 7m (20ft) long and weigh more than 2 tonnes. The female or cow is only half the size of the bull. Elephant seals belong to the group of seals known as the earless seals.

Seals are carnivores with a difference. Most carnivores live on land. Seals, however, live in the water, coming on land only to rest and to breed. There are some seals that actually mate in water but even so, the females have to come on land to give birth to their young, which are called pups.

When seals come out on land in large numbers to mate and to give birth, those places where they do so are called *rookeries*.

Millions of years ago the ancestors of seals lived on land. Then they took to living in water. This meant that their bodies had to undergo many changes. Their limbs changed from legs to flippers and they lost their tails – only a stump of it now remains. As they changed to living in water, their diet changed, too. They started eating fish and other water animals, such as squid, octopus and shellfish.

Seals are divided into three families: the earless seals, eared seals and walruses. But even the eared seals have only tiny ear flaps.

The earless seals
Earless seals are also called true seals or hair seals. The smallest of them is the one known in Britain as the common seal and in North America as the harbor seal. It is 2m (6½ft) long. The largest is the sea elephant or elephant seal, which lives in Antarctic waters. The male elephant seal is 6.5m (20ft) long and weighs 2 tonnes (2¼ tons). True seals have a harsh dark fur but, with the exception of the harbor seal, which is born with the adult coat, their pups have pale woolly coats.

Eared seals
There are two kinds of eared seals: the sea lions and the fur seals. One way in which they differ from true seals is that they can bring their hind flippers forward, to use them for walking on land. The true seals cannot do this and can only move clumsily when on land. The fur seals used to be killed in large numbers when sealskin fur coats were fashionable.

Walruses

Walruses are found only in Arctic seas. They used to haul out, as the saying goes, onto beaches, like other seals. Now, because so many were killed for their ivory tusks, their oil and their flesh, they haul out mainly on icefloes.

Male walruses may be 4m (13ft) long and weigh about 1 tonne. The females are only 2.5m (8ft) long. A walrus' skin is wrinkled and has only short fur. As it grows older it loses most of its fur, so that its skin is more or less naked.

What makes a walrus different from other seals is its long tusks. These are long canine teeth that hang down from the upper jaw. The tusks are made of a kind of ivory. Walruses eat mainly clams and crabs. It used to be said that they used their tusks for digging up the seabed in their search for food. It is now known this is not so, but no one knows what purpose the tusks do serve.

▶ Walruses live in the Arctic regions of both the Atlantic and the Pacific Oceans. They form the third family of seals and they, too, are earless. Both males and females have a pair of large tusks.

▼ For hundreds of years, in India and south-east Asia, elephants have been tamed and used as beasts of burden. An elephant may live for 70 years, so the man who trains it will probably ride it all its life.

ELEPHANTS

There are two kinds of elephant living today. One is called the Indian elephant, although it is also found in forests throughout south-east Asia. The other is the African elephant, now found mainly in tropical Africa.

The Indian elephant is the smaller, up to 3m (10ft) in height and weighing up to 4 tonnes (4½ tons). It has smaller ears than the African. Its forehead is high and domed and there is only one lip at the end of its trunk. It has five nails on each front foot and four on each hind foot. Its trunk is smooth and its back is ridged and convex. Only the male has tusks and even these are small. This is the elephant usually seen in zoos and it is the one that is tamed and used for dragging heavy loads.

The African elephant is up to 3½m (11ft) high and weighs up to 6 tonnes (6½ tons). It has large flapping ears, its forehead is sloping and there are two lips at the end of the trunk. It has four nails on each front foot and three on each hind foot. The trunk is ringed and the back is hollow (concave). The males and females both have long tusks, up to 2m (6½ft) long.

The useful trunk

An elephant's long trunk is really its nose. Its eyes are very small and it has poor sight, but its sense of smell is very good. It also uses its trunk rather like a hand. It can grasp food with its trunk to put into its mouth. It can suck up water with the trunk and squirt it into its mouth to drink or spray it over its body to take a bath. It will also use the trunk to suck up dust to blow it over its body, to take a dust bath.

Tusks and teeth

Its tusks are elongated incisor teeth growing from the upper jaw. They are used to attack enemies. They are also used for levering up small trees, digging up roots and boring into the ground for water. Other than these, an elephant has only a simple large molar on each side of both upper and lower jaw. An elephant's food is tough: leaves, young branches and ripe fruit. These are hard on the teeth. As the first molars wear out they are pushed out by others growing behind them. This happens five times during an elephant's life, as if the molars were on a conveyor belt system. When the last molars are worn out the elephant can no longer feed and so will die. This usually happens at about 50 years of age.

◀ An elephant's trunk has many uses. This baby elephant (the hairs on its skin show very clearly) is spraying itself with water to keep cool. With its trunk it can smell ripening fruit a mile or more away and it can suck up water for drinking.

◀ There are four
species of hyrax. They
are also known as
dassies, coneys or rock-
rabbits. They are found
from Syria and Arabia
to South Africa. About
the size of a rabbit, a
hyrax looks like a kind
of rodent, but it is
really an ungulate.
Even more surprising
it is probably distantly
related to the
elephants.

▲ Elephants at a
waterhole in Africa.
The largest land
animals now living,
elephants are related
to the long extinct
mammoths and
mastodons.

THE HORSE FAMILY

◄ A group of wild horses grazing among the tall grasses that are their chief food. Like other herbivores, horses have back teeth with wide ridged surfaces to help grind down the tough vegetation on which they feed.

There was a time when wild horses could be found in large numbers in Europe and Asia. Today only a few are left. Prehistoric man killed them for food or caught them and made them work for him. The only truly wild horse now left is the Mongolian wild horse.

The two other kinds of animal that make up the horse family are the ass and the zebra. Wild asses used to be common in the deserts of North Africa and

▲ The shading of the coat of the Somali wild ass helps it blend well with the rocky areas where it lives.

► Zebras are very like horses in all but one thing: the way their coat is striped. The two shown here are a mare and foal of Burchell's zebra. This is the commonest species of zebra and is found throughout eastern and southern Africa.

southern Asia. Their domesticated descendants, the donkeys, are still common, but wild asses are now quite rare.

It is much the same story for the zebras, or striped horses, as they have been called. Until the end of the nineteenth century, zebras could be seen by the tens of thousands on the plains of Africa. They were killed for their flesh and their hides or just for sport.

Disappearing toes

These three animals, the horses, asses and zebras, are called odd-toed *ungulates*. Each of their four legs ends in a single hoof which is nothing more than an enlarged toe-nail. The first horses, those that lived millions of years ago, had four toes on the front feet and three toes on each hind foot. As time passed one toe on each foot became longer and stronger than the rest and the nail on it grew into a hoof. At the same time the side toes grew weaker. Today, under the skin of the lower part of a horse's leg, are the remains of these outer toes. They are called splint bones.

Very rarely, a foal is born with three toes on each foot. This is a throw-back, a reminder of what some of its ancestors used to have. It is useful to know about this because it helps us to understand why scientists classify tapirs as close relatives of the horses, asses and zebras.

Tapirs

A tapir is about the size of a donkey, except that its legs are short and it is only about 1m (3½ft) at the shoulder. It has only a stump of a tail but its snout is long and flexible, making it rather similar to the upper lip of a horse. Like some of the prehistoric horses, it has four hoof-like nails on each front foot and three on each hind foot.

Another way in which horses and tapirs are alike is in their teeth. Both have flat-crowned molars for eating plant food. Plants have fibres which must be ground down before being swallowed and the flat-crowned molars grind these, just as grain is ground between millstones to give flour.

Tapirs live in two quite separate parts of the world: south-east Asia and tropical regions of South America. The different species are very similar, except that the Malayan tapir has black and white markings. These act as excellent camouflage in the sunlight and shade of the forests in which it lives. The South American species are mainly blackish-brown.

▲ Of the five species of tapir, one lives in Malaya the others in South America. Those in South America are brown or black all over except for grey or white patches on the head and chest. Tapirs are good swimmers and can even swim underwater.

RHINOCEROSES

► Indian rhinos are now found only in Nepal and Assam, although once they were found over a much wider area. Like the white rhino (**opposite**), they are peaceful plant-eating animals.

◄ The hide of the great Indian rhino is thrown into folds, which makes the animal look as if it were armour-plated. In spite of its appearance it is inoffensive, except to tigers, its only natural enemy.

The rhinoceros is another plant-feeder that has teeth similar to those of a horse. It also has an odd number of toes, each one ending in a hoof-like nail. So it, too, is classed as an odd-toed ungulate.

There are five species of rhinoceros. All of them are now rare and in danger of extinction. Although they are all bulky animals with short legs, they are able to run fairly fast.

They have poor sight but a keen sense of smell. When a rhinoceros charges it can reach a speed of 55kph (35mph), and its great weight is enough to make it dangerous. It also has on its snout one, sometimes two, dangerous-looking horns. This horn is unlike the horns of cattle and deer. It is made of horny fibres and used to be described as being made up of matted hair. This is a good way of thinking of it.

Rhinoceroses are one of the largest land animals after the elephants. The largest of them, the square-lipped rhino or white rhino, of Africa, weighs 4 tonnes (4½ tons). The next in size is the great Indian rhino, 2½ tonnes (2½ tons). Then come the black rhino of Africa and the Javan rhino, both 1½ tonnes (1½ tons) and finally the Sumatran rhino, ½ tonne (½ ton).

Really thick skins

The skin of all rhinos, except the Sumatran, is hairless apart from a brush of bristles on the tip of the tail and fringes of hair on the ears. The Sumatran rhino has long but rather scanty hair on the body. The skin of the great Indian and Javan rhinos, in particular, is very thick. It grows into folds and looks like armour-plating. But because of their thick skins, all rhinos can rush through the thorny thickets of the regions in which they live without hurting themselves.

▲ Wallowing in muddy water is something Indian rhinos seem to thoroughly enjoy. Sometimes groups of about ten will wallow together. Although protected because they are one of the world's endangered animals, rhinos are still hunted and killed illegally.

► The white rhinoceros, the largest of the five species of rhino, is usually light grey. The black rhinoceros is usually dark grey. The one pictured here is a white rhino. Although they look fierce, they are quite peaceful animals, and feed quietly on leaves and grass.

HIPPOS AND PIGS

▲ The pygmy hippo lives either alone or in pairs in forest streams in West Africa. It is much smaller than the common hippo: 1.6m (5ft) long, 80cm (2ft 8in) at the shoulder and weighing 270kg (600lb).

The hippopotamus

The next largest ungulate, after the great Indian rhinoceros, is the common hippopotamus, which may weigh as much as $3\frac{1}{2}$ tonnes ($3\frac{1}{2}$ tons). It is one of the even-toed ungulates, and has four toes on each foot, each toe ending in a hoof-like nail.

The hippopotamus, or river horse as it is sometimes called, is found only in Africa. It has a huge barrel-like body supported by short stumpy legs and an enormous head. It spends most of the day in water, or lying asleep on a sandbank. At night it comes out on land to feed on tall grass along the river banks.

The eyes and ears of a hippo are on top of the head. So the animal can keep watch for enemies, lying low in the water with only the eyes and ears showing. If anything comes near it the hippo will open its huge mouth and show its long tusks. This is not a yawn. When the hippo opens its mouth wide it is showing that it is prepared to fight. It can inflict terrible wounds with its tusks. Large crocodiles are its main enemies, but hippos also fight among themselves. When they do this each tries to break the other's foreleg. A hippo with a broken leg cannot support its great weight on land, so it cannot feed and will die.

The other kind of hippo, the pygmy hippo, is very much smaller – just as its name suggests. It is only about 1.5m (5ft) long, compared with the common hippo's length of up to 4.5m (14ft).

▼ Two female hippopotamuses lying side-by-side in the water. Two hammerhead storks find they make a good perch. Herds of hippopotamus used to be common in rivers and lakes from the Nile delta in Egypt to the Cape in South Africa. Today, they are not found north of Khartoum in the Sudan nor south of the Zambezi River, in Zambia, except in national parks.

Members of the pig family

Another ferocious even-toed ungulate is the peccary or wild pig of tropical America. This is a distant cousin of the hippo and of the farmyard pig or hog. Peccaries look like pigs except that they have a coat of stiffer bristles and a larger head. They live in herds, eating any plants or animal they can find. When attacked they will go into holes in the ground. If they cannot do this they turn to face the enemy, champing their tusks and charging in a group.

There are half-a-dozen species of wild pig in Europe, Asia and Africa. The European wild boar is the one that was domesticated to become the farmyard pig. It spends its time rooting in the ground eating anything, plant or animal, it can find. It will also browse on green leaves. The Indian crested boar is like the wild boar except for a crest of black bristles from the back of its head to the shoulders. Both these wild pigs have razor-sharp tusks which they will use to defend themselves if threatened. The crested boar has been known to fight even a tiger.

The largest wild pig is the giant forest hog of Kenya. It stands 80cm (32in) at the shoulder and can weigh up to 136kg (300lb). The smallest is the pygmy hog of Nepal. It is only 30cm (1ft) high. The babirusa, the wild pig of the island of Celebes in the south-west Pacific Ocean, is about the same height, but has long legs and looks more like a deer. It is also nearly hairless.

▼ A group of wild boar piglets in a swampy area of northern Italy. Their striped coats help them blend with the vegetation of their surroundings.

▶ The collared peccary is the wild pig of tropical America. It grows to about 1m (3ft) in length and weighs up to 25kg (50lb). Wild pigs are distantly related to the hippopotamuses. Peccaries live in herds among thick scrub and feed on fruits, roots and almost any plant or animal they can find.

CAMELS

Everyone knows that a camel is an animal with a hump, that lives in deserts and can go for days without drinking. It used also to be said that a camel stored water in its hump. This is not true. Fat is stored in the hump.

The camel is also called the ship of the desert, because, so it is said, it is able to carry loads across deserts where other animals would die of thirst. It is also able to live by eating the dry thorns found in deserts.

A camel's feet are also adapted to desert conditions. It has two toes on each foot. Each toe has a hoof-like nail. This makes it a *cloven*-hoofed ungulate. The soles of its feet are padded, so they do not slip or sink in sand.

The best-known camel is the one-humped camel. It is also called the Arabian camel and is used in large

▶ The only other species of camel still living is the Bactrian or two-humped camel, of Central Asia. It is not as tall as the Arabian but is heavier. There are wild camels of this species in the Gobi desert. They are a little different from the domesticated Bactrian camels, with smaller humps and a coat of much shorter, sandy coloured hair.

numbers in North Africa and Arabia. None of them is found in the wild today, except where they have escaped and gone wild. The one-humped camel is sometimes called a dromedary. Strictly speaking a dromedary is a special type of camel used for riding.

The only other kind of camel is the two-humped camel, or Bactrian camel, of Central Asia. This is much more hairy than the one-humped camel, with patches of long hair on its head and neck. The Bactrian camel is used for carrying heavy loads. A few wild Bactrian camels still survive in the Gobi desert.

▼ Arabian camels have been used for centuries as beasts of burden. A camel will carry a load of 272kg (600lb) and make long journeys without drinking. One camel train went six days without water. When there is no water, plants wetted with dew provide a little moisture.

▼ A young vicuña, one of the South American animals related to the camel. Like the alpaca, the coat of the vicuña is fine and soft and used to make cloth.

South American camels

Llamas are relatives of the camel that live in South America. A llama does not have a hump but, like the camel, it has a long neck and two toes on each foot. It also has a long woolly coat. Again, like a camel, a llama can go for days without water and with little food. So it is used as a beast of burden in the deserts and semi-deserts of South America.

A special kind of llama is known as the alpaca. Its coat is made up of very fine long wool from which a soft, expensive cloth is made. It is bred specially for its wool.

On the southern plains of South America lives the wild guanaco, in herds of about a hundred. The guanaco is smaller than the llama, only 120cm (4ft) to the top of its head. It, too, is related to the camel but has no hump. Even smaller, and only 100cm (3ft) tall, is the vicuña that lives high up in the Andes mountains. It has even been found above the snowline at 5,400m (18,000ft).

Millions of years ago there were wild camels of many kinds in both North and South America. Today the guanaco and the vicuña are the only wild species left in the whole of the American continent.

▼ Llamas live in high open country – not desert regions as camels do.

THE DEER FAMILY

▲ A female roe deer stands alert on the edge of woodlands. If danger threatens, the deer will disappear swiftly and silently into the woods.

◄ Fallow deer belong to Europe and south-west Asia. They used to be very numerous in the wild, but hunting and the clearance of woods and forests have reduced their number. The buck (male) is 1m (3ft) at the shoulder. The doe (female) is slightly smaller.

▶ Twice a year caribou in Canada make a trek between summer and winter feeding grounds. Caribou are the North American equivalents of the reindeer in Europe. They are larger than reindeer and start breeding slightly earlier in the year.

Deer are cloven-hoofed animals that have antlers on their heads, although usually it is only the males that have them. The antlers, which are usually branched, are shed and fresh ones grown each year.

Then, each time a new set is regrown the antlers have a greater number of branches. So antlers are unlike the horns of cattle which are not shed each year.

Now we come to another of those exceptions to the rules which makes classifying animals so difficult: not all deer have antlers! But they are still classified as deer because there are no other important differences in their anatomy.

The small musk deer of Asia have no antlers. Instead they have long upper canine teeth that form tusks. The musk deer use these in fighting.

The muntjac or barking deer, of south-east Asia, also has tusk-like canines. But it also has a pair of small antlers.

The Chinese water deer has neither tusks nor antlers. When in danger it scuttles through grass like a rabbit and then drops flat on the ground out of sight.

None of these deer is more than 60cm (2ft) tall. But they are not the smallest deer. The pudu of South America is even smaller. This is only 37cm (15in) high and has very tiny spikes for antlers.

The largest deer is the moose that lives in the marshy forests of North America. It is 2.5m (nearly 8ft) high. The male moose has enormous antlers spanning nearly 2m (6½ft). But here we come to a mix-up in names. In Europe a deer almost identical with the moose is known as an elk. But in North America the name elk is given to a deer almost identical with the red deer of Europe and Asia. The animal known as the American elk is also called a wapiti. This is its Red Indian name.

Most deer are forest dwellers. They will eat grass but most of them prefer the leaves of bushes and shrubs. What is

more, if they have only grass to eat they do not grow as large as those able to feed on leaves and their antlers do not grow as large.

Deer of the far north

In Northern Europe and Asia lives the reindeer. This has been domesticated by the people living in these cold regions. The Lapps, for instance, used to depend on the reindeer for almost everything. They kept them in herds, milked the females, ate the flesh of the reindeer, used its hide for clothes and making their wigwam-like dwellings and used the living deer to pull their sleighs.

When people from Europe settled in North America they found deer that looked like the reindeer except that they were bigger. The American Indians called these deer caribou.

Not only do reindeer and caribou look alike, they feed alike. In winter, when snow covers the ground, both scrape away the snow to eat the lichens, called reindeer moss. Reindeer and caribou are also unusual among deer because the females, as well as the males, have antlers.

◄ A young bull moose browses on sprouting shoots in the short spring in northern Canada.

▼ Reindeer and caribou are well adapted to the arctic conditions of the areas where they live. They have thick coats and hoofs that splay out as they touch the ground, so that the feet do not sink into the snow.

SHEEP AND GOATS

▶ A flock of Merino sheep in Australia. One reason why sheep were favoured for domestication is that they follow each other and so keep together. This makes it easy for the farmer to look after them.

Wild sheep and goats live in barren and precipitous places. Although related to domestic sheep their coats are hairy, never woolly. Except for the Barbary sheep, all wild sheep and goats have small tails.

The home of the mouflon, the only European wild sheep, is in the mountains of the mediterranean islands of Corsica and Sardinia. It stands 67cm (27in) at the shoulder. At one time it was hunted for the heavy horns that curve in a spiral each side of its head. The largest and finest of all wild sheep is the argali. This lives in the mountains of Central Asia.

The rams have massive spiral horns, with wrinkled surfaces. A large ram has such big horns that it needs specially strong muscles to support their weight. The ewes' horns are short, straight and thin.

The only wild sheep in America is the bighorn or Rocky Mountain sheep, which is over 1m (3½ft) at the shoulder. It has a tawny-buff coat with a striking white patch on the rump. Its spiral horns are smoother than in most sheep.

Goats are noted for being sure-footed, able to leap about among rocks. They can also survive in regions where there is only scanty vegetation. Wild goats include the ibexes and markhors. Their horns are often of great length. They either curve upwards and backwards in a sabre-like sweep or are spirally twisted, like corkscrews. Goats' horns never grow out from the sides of the head, as sheeps' horns do. The males have a beard and give off a strong scent. Both sexes have horns.

There are five species of ibex in the mountains of the Mediterranean region and Asia. They are wild goats with sweeping curved horns, flattened from side-to-side with a row of large knobs on the front edge. The largest is the ibex of the Himalayas and Siberia. This stands 1m (3½ft) at the shoulder with horns 1.5m (5ft) long. The horns of the females are small and slender.

Markhors, another type of wild goat,

▼ Semi-wild sheep do not have the fleecy coats of domesticated sheep. They have an outer coat of long hair and beneath this is a fine undercoat of wool.

52

also live in the Himalayas. They have
corkscrew horns and a large beard that
continues down the throat and chest.

Goat-antelopes

Goat-antelopes is a name used for several
goat-like animals. They all have short
horns. The best-known goat-antelope is
the chamois which is remarkable for the
skill with which it is able to leap about
the most rocky mountainsides.

A most unusual relative of goats is the
musk-ox. This lives in herds and could be
mistaken for cattle. It is over 1.5m (5ft)
at the shoulder, has a shaggy coat
reaching nearly to the ground and huge
curved horns shaped rather like butchers'
meat hooks. Its home is in the Canadian
Arctic and in Greenland.

▼ Sheep were
domesticated several
thousand years ago.
The only wild sheep
left in Europe is the
mouflon, which lives in
the mountains of
Corsica, Sardinia and
Cyprus.

► The markhor is a
wild goat living in the
Himalaya mountains.
Both males and
females have a long
beard and mane but
only the male has the
magnificent spiral
horns.

A giant among animals

The first giraffes to reach the zoos of Europe and North America caused quite a stir. This is hardly surprising as there is no other animal quite like the giraffe.

To begin with, a giraffe is nearly 6m (18ft) tall, three times the height of a tall man. It has long legs and, more remarkable still, a long tapering neck. Set on top of the neck is a small head with several short horns. Some giraffes have only two horns, others have three or

Although a giraffe has such a long neck it cannot reach down to drink without straddling its front legs wide apart and bending its knees to reach the water. But the long neck comes in useful for reaching up to pluck leaves from tall trees that other animals cannot reach. The giraffe plucks the leaves by wrapping its long tongue around them to pull them into its mouth.

The great height of a giraffe also has another use. It is like a watchtower from eyes, see its enemies from a long way away.

Although it looks clumsy a giraffe is very graceful when running. It does not move its legs as most other four-legged animals do. Instead it moves the legs on one side together, then the legs on the other side. This makes it sway as it runs, but it can move fast across the plains of southern Africa where it lives.

The giraffe's long legs end in large cloven hoofs. A kick from a giraffe will kill a lion.

The body of a giraffe is covered with chestnut or dark brown blotches separated by paler, buff lines. These break up the outline of its body. So, when the animal is standing among tall trees it is very hard to see.

A smaller relative

In the rain forests of West Africa lives the giraffe's smaller cousin, the okapi. Its coat is a rich plummy purple with white bands on its legs. In the gloom of the dense forests the okapi is very hard to find. As a result, it was not discovered by white men until 1900, although the African hunters knew where to find it. Okapis live solitary lives, which makes them even harder to find. This is unlike giraffes that live in groups of six or more and can be seen from afar, if they are not standing among tall trees.

▼ The okapi is about the size of a horse. Yet until 1900 it was unknown except to the pygmy tribes living in the Ituri Forest, in West Africa. In the gloom of this tropical forest, among dense undergrowth, the plum-coloured coat and striped legs of the okapi seem to melt into the background.

WILD CATTLE

Herds of cows and bulls are found on farms wherever there are grassy plains. They are called cattle. There are also wild cattle and their relatives, the buffaloes. All are heavily-built animals that eat grass. They chew the cud. That is, they crop the grass and, without chewing, swallow it. Later they bring it back into their mouths a little at a time, and chew it properly.

Both the females and the males have horns that curve sideways and upwards. These are not like the antlers of deer, which are also animals that chew the cud. In cattle, each horn is made up of a core of bone covered with horn.

The wild ox of Europe, Asia and North Africa, known as the aurochs, died out in 1627. It was a large powerful animal 2m (6½ft) high at the shoulder. Most farm cattle are descended from it.

The gaur, of India, another species of wild cattle, is even larger – the bulls weigh up to 900kg (2,000lb). Yet, although so large, it rarely attacks, preferring to retire into the woods when disturbed.

Is it a buffalo or a bison?

Another animal of the same family is the European bison, also known as the wisent. It used to live in forests with the aurochs but only a few are now left. These are protected in a forest in Poland.

The second species of bison is the more famous. This is the American buffalo. It is not a true buffalo, although it has always been given that name since settlers from Europe first saw it. One hundred years ago the western plains of the United States and Canada were said to be dark with the herds of buffalo. The buffaloes were there in their millions. Now only a few thousand are left – carefully protected.

The real buffalo

True buffalo are found in Africa and India. The African buffalo stands over

▲ The aurochs, the ancestor of modern domestic cattle became extinct in 1627. At Munich zoo, scientists have bred animals that are like the original aurochs.

▼ The North American buffalo has a massive head and forequarters covered with shaggy hair. A well-grown buffalo may be 3.5m (11ft) long, its tail 60cm (2ft) long and its weight well over 1 tonne (1 ton).

▼ A zebu or Brahma bull has large ears and folds of loose skin around the throat. These help it to lose body heat and so keep cool in the hot season in India where it lives.

1.5m (5ft) at the shoulder. It has wide spreading horns and is very dangerous. A herd of African buffalo has been seen killing a lion. They tossed the lion from one buffalo to another, on their horns, until it was dead.

The Indian buffalo, or water buffalo, is a black powerful animal, which also has long wide-spreading horns. It lives in swampy ground and spends much time wallowing. It is much used as a domestic beast of burden and is very docile. However, if they scent a tiger Indian buffaloes will attack in a body and trample it into the ground.

The yak thrives on the bleak plateaux of central Asia. It can survive on the barest and coarsest vegetation. The yak is noted for its long black hair hanging almost to the ground. The domesticated yak provides meat and milk as well as being used as a beast of burden. Its only enemy is the wolf. When wolves are about the parent yak form a circle with the calves inside to protect them.

▲ Probably the most dreaded animal in Africa is the Cape buffalo. It fears nothing. By day it likes to lie up in swampy reed beds or in lakes. It takes a drink in the evening and then feeds during the night in herds that may number a thousand. The Cape buffalo is just over 2m (7ft) long, stands 1.5m (5ft) at the shoulder and weighs a tonne (1 ton) or more.

▼ Although the musk-ox looks like a species of cattle, it is one of the goat-antelopes (page 53). It lives in herds in the arctic regions of Canada and Greenland. When attacked the herd stands shoulder to shoulder to face the enemy. This is successful against wolves but useless against men with rifles.

ANTELOPES AND GAZELLES

► Throughout eastern Africa, from Kenya southwards, lives the suni. It is the smallest of all antelopes, little more than 30cm (1ft) at the shoulder. When disturbed, it bolts for cover in the grass and scrub. Although so small it can leap 3m (10ft) to make its escape.

The antelopes, like cattle, are *ruminants*. Some of the smaller species, especially those of delicate build, are called gazelles. Antelopes include those ruminants that are not deer, cattle, sheep or goats. The smallest, the duiker, is no larger than a hare. The largest, the eland, is as big if not bigger than the largest ox. In some species only the males have horns. In other species both sexes have them. The horns may be long or short, straight or spiral, curving forwards or curving backwards.

The way they live is also very varied. The small duikers scuttle about in the grass. The klipspringer, about the size of a medium-sized dog, has small hoofs and can scramble over bare rocks or leap onto a small pinnacle of rock and stay poised there with all four feet close together.

Antelopes represent one of the wonders of the world. When white men began to explore the continent of Africa, south of the Sahara desert, they found the countryside filled with uncountable millions of antelopes. The wonder was not only that there were so many different kinds but that they all found a living there.

Food for all

Since all antelopes feed on plants, it seemed amazing that the many millions of them did not eat up all the vegetation, leaving the ground bare. We now know that each species of antelope eats a different part of the plant, or eats it at a different time of the year. In this way they do not compete with each other for the available food.

A good example of how antelopes avoid competition is shown by the gerenuk. It has a long neck and long legs and has learnt to stand on its hind legs to reach up for the foliage of trees that other antelopes cannot reach.

The speedy pronghorn

Antelopes are also found in southern Asia, and there is one species in America. It is called the pronghorned antelope, or pronghorn for short. According to scientists it is not a true antelope. Unlike other antelopes it sheds its horns once a year, so it is classified in a family of its own. Pronghorns are the fastest of all ruminants, and have reached speeds of over 66kph (40mph).

◄ Except for the shape of the horns, eland could be mistaken for cattle. They are the largest of all antelopes, standing 2m (6½ft) at the shoulder. The horns are straight, directed backwards and have spiral ridges on the lower half.

► The dainty Peter's gazelle is a good example of the antelopes known as gazelles. It lives on the plains of Africa, well away from cover to avoid being ambushed by lions. It stands just over 60cm (2ft) at the shoulder and its horns can be up to 60cm (2ft) long.

▲ Probably the most showy of all antelopes is the nyala. It lives in a small area of southeast Africa. The coat of the male is chestnut and black, marked with white spots and stripes. The does, which are bright foxred with white stripes, do not have horns.

► Most famous of antelopes, and also the most swift, the blackbuck lives on the open plains of India. It stands 80cm (32in) at the shoulder. For centuries it has been used for sport, being chased by tame cheetahs belonging to the Indian princes.

WHALES, DOLPHINS AND PORPOISES

► The blue whale, the largest animal that has ever lived, is a whalebone whale. The plates of whalebone can be seen hanging from its upper jaw. Whalebone whales swim through shoals of krill near the ocean's surface, with their mouths open, straining the krill from the water.

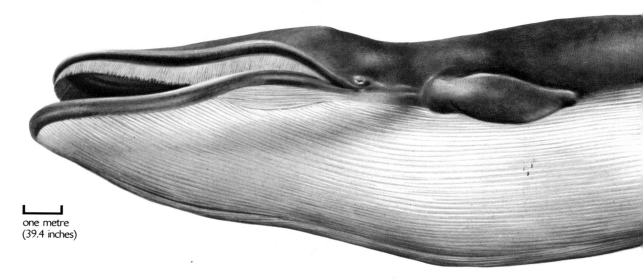

one metre
(39.4 inches)

Whales were once known as 'great fish'. This was because both fish and whales spend all their lives in the water, but they are not related in any way. Both have streamlined bodies but whereas a fish swims by wagging its tail from side-to-side, a whale swims by wagging its tail up-and-down.

Another important difference between whales and fishes is that whales, because they are mammals, are warm-blooded and fishes are cold-blooded. Yet both live all their lives in water and would die if they left the water to come onto land. Although the water is cold, whales are able to keep warm because they have a thick layer of oily *blubber* under their very thin skin. They have no hair except a few bristles on the snout and these are usually found only in the young.

Many millions of years ago whales lived on land. They then had four legs. We know this because all whales have tiny hip bones and very occasionally a whale is born with small hind legs. Although their front legs have changed to flippers, the bones in them are very like those in our arms and hands.

A whale has no neck but it still has seven neck bones – the same number as most mammals. Another thing that marks a whale as a mammal is that its young is born alive and is fed with its mother's milk. As soon as a baby whale is born it swims to the surface to take its first gulp of air to fill its lungs. Often the mother will help it by putting her snout under it to lift it to the surface. Then the baby swims beside its mother.

The mother whale has no teats. Instead she has two slits in her *abdomen* through which she squirts milk into her baby's mouth as it swims close to her.

Whales are divided into two groups. These are the toothed whales and the whalebone whales. Toothed whales feed on squid and fish. They have peg-like teeth which in the sperm whale may be 20cm (8in) long. Whalebone whales have no teeth. Instead they have plates of whalebone hanging down from the roof of the mouth. These are used to strain small fish and small prawns, known as *krill*, from the sea. The blue, fin and humpback whales all belong to this group.

The largest whale is the blue whale. It may reach a length of 30m (100ft) or more and may weigh 142 tonnes (140 tons). It is the largest animal that has ever lived. The smallest whale is the La Plata dolphin that lives in the estuary of the Rio de la Plata, in South America. It is only 1.60m (5ft) long.

The small whales are called dolphins and porpoises. Most whales live in the sea, but some of the dolphins live in the large rivers. The home of the Chinese river dolphin, for example, is in Tung Ting Lake, nearly 1,000km (600miles) up the Yangtze river valley.

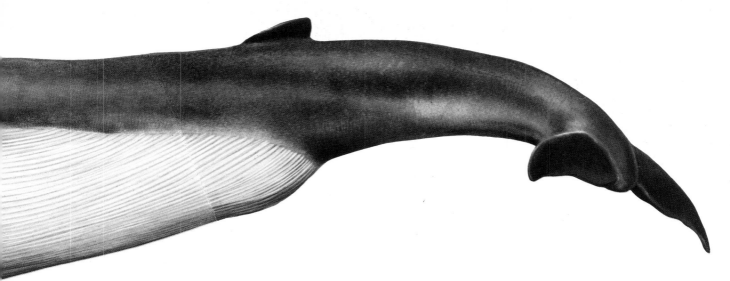

► The back of a fin whale breaks the ocean surface. Fin whales belong to the group of whales known as the whalebone or baleen whales.

▲ Dolphins are strong swimmers, their stream-lined shape and smooth flexible skin help to reduce water-resistance to a minimum.

► Close-up of a dolphin's blow-hole, as it comes to the surface to breathe. Under the water, the blow-hole is closed by a special muscle to stop water entering.

GLOSSARY

Abdomen The part of the body in which the stomach and intestines are found.

Blubber The thick oily layer beneath the skin of a whale.

Canine A single tooth that occurs after the incisors on each side of the upper and lower jaws of most mammals. These teeth are particularly well developed in the dog family. Canine can also be used to describe a dog or something that has the characteristics of a dog.

Carnassials Strong, well-developed teeth used for cutting flesh.

Carnivore An animal that eats flesh.

Classify To arrange in groups, each member of the group being related to the other members. Scientists arrange (classify) animals into groups to show the relationship between them.

Cloven Literally this means split. The feet of such animals as deer, cattle and pigs are described as cloven because there appears to be a deep slit between the two parts of each foot.

Cold-blooded Term used to describe an animal whose body temperature varies according to the temperature of the surrounding air.

Cusp Point on the surface of a tooth.

Echo-location A means of locating objects used by bats. They send out high-pitched sounds which are reflected back from any nearby objects as echoes. The bats can tell from the echoes where the objects are.

Edentates Mammals belonging to the group known as Edentata or toothless ones.

Ermine The winter coat of the stoat which is white except for the black tip to the tail.

Filament A long thin thread.

Follicle Small cavity in the surface of the skin from which hairs grow.

Herbivore An animal that eats plants.

Hibernate/hibernation The state in which some animals pass the winter. The heart and breathing rate slow down, the body temperature drops and the animal becomes cold-blooded. The animal goes into a form of very deep sleep.

Incisors Front teeth in the jaws of most mammals.

Insectivore An animal that eats mainly insects.

Insulation A form of protection against something that could be harmful. The blubber of a whale insulates (protects) the rest of its body against cold sea temperatures.

Krill Tiny sea creatures eaten by some whales.

Lagomorph Mammal belonging to the group known as Lagomorpha, which includes rabbits and hares.

Mammal An animal which is fed on its mother's milk while it is a baby.

Marsupial Group of mammals in which the females carry their babies in a pouch.

Molars Back teeth in some mammals, used for grinding.

► A group of bats hibernating in a cave during the winter.

◀ Of all land mammals, only elephants are larger than the white rhino which lives on the lowland plains of southern Africa.

Nectar A sweet fluid found in flowers.

Nose-leaves Folds of skin on the faces of some species of bat.

Pentadactyl Foot with five fingers (or toes). All mammals have feet like this, even though they may be flippers (seals and whales) or hooves (horses).

Pollen Tiny grains from the stamens of flowers that fertilize the seeds.

Premolars Teeth that come in front of the molars.

Primates Group of mammals which includes lemurs, monkeys, apes and men.

Quill Very long spine found in the coat of animals such as the porcupine.

Reptiles Cold-blooded animals such as tortoises, snakes and crocodiles.

Retractile Term used to describe the claws of cats which can be extended or drawn back into sheaths.

Rogue A wild animal that suddenly and unusually behaves in a vicious, bad-tempered way. Such animals are highly dangerous and are usually driven out of the herd or group to which they had belonged.

Rookery Place on land where seals come to mate and have their babies.

Ruminant An animal that chews the cud.

Ungulate One of the hoofed mammals.

Vertebrae The bones that make up the backbone or spine.

Vertebrate An animal with a backbone.

Warm-blooded Term used to describe an animal whose body remains at an almost constant temperature, whatever the temperature of the surrounding air.

◀ Manatees are large herbivorous water mammals. They live in the rivers and on the coasts of tropical America, the West Indies and West Africa. Like whales they have a layer of blubber beneath the skin.

INDEX

Acknowledgements

Ardea, Australia House, Baschieri, Ian Beames, Ron Boardman, A Borgioli and G Cappelli, Camera Press, N Cirani, Bruce Coleman, SG Costa, EPS, S Ferri-Ricchi, L Gaggero, Prof Dr Lutz Heck, Eric Hosking, Archivio IGDA, Jacana, Keystone, Frank Lane, London Zoological Society, Archivio Longo, A Margiocco, Marka, P Morris, Norman Myers/Afrique Photo, NHPA, Nature Photographers, Novosti, T Okapia, Ostman, L Pellegrini, S Prato, JR Simon, J Six, Spectrum Colour Library, C Venturini, ZEFA.